A New BOOK of 5 RINGS

Essential tactics for today's leader

ADAPTED FROM
THE SENSEI LEADER
BY JIM BOUCHARD

San Chi Publishing
2018

© 2018 by Jim Bouchard

Booking for speaking, corporate training and media appearances available through **Black Belt Mindset Productions.**

TheSenseiLeader.com

Cover & book design by **Diego Designs**

All rights reserved. No portion of this book may be reproduced, stored in a retrieval system, or transmitted in any form or by any means, electronic, mechanical, photocopy, recording or scanning, or otherwise without written permission of the author and publisher—except for brief quotations in critical reviews or articles.

Published in the United States of America by **San Chi Publishing**

First printing: February 2018

ISBN-13: 978-1985820791

ISBN-10: 198582079X

A MAN CANNOT UNDERSTAND
THE ART HE IS STUDYING
IF HE ONLY LOOKS FOR
THE END RESULT WITHOUT
TAKING THE TIME TO
DELVE DEEPLY INTO THE
REASONING OF THE STUDY.

~MYAMOTO MUSASHI

Contents

PREFACE: YOU LEAD PEOPLE! I

INTRODUCTION: MUSASHI AND THE ORIGINAL 5 RINGS 1

5 RINGS = 5 TACTICS 13

THE 5 RINGS 27

THE COMMENTARIES 39

   Opposition 41

   Deflection 47

   Leverage 55

   Borrowing 61

   Harmony 67

APPLICATION 69

FINAL WORD—AND IT'S A WORD OF CAUTION 77

PREFACE: YOU LEAD PEOPLE!

The first thing I want to make clear is—this isn't a book full of answers. It's a book meant to inspire questions. My intention is to provoke some thought.

> *Are you using these tactics in your life as a leader?*
>
> *Are you using them effectively?*
>
> *Can you find more uses for them?*
>
> *Do you need more practice or study?*

Next, you don't need to be a martial artist to understand these tactics or make use of them.

My own interest in martial arts did not start with any particular interest in self-defense. I didn't pursue martial arts to learn to defend my life from some outside aggressor.

A New Book of 5 Rings

My mission was to save my own life—from *my own self!*

I began my study of martial arts to help me stay off drugs and to overcome a debilitating lack of self-worth and self-confidence.

My interest was far more engaged by the philosophy rather than the physicality of the arts. I enjoyed the physical part of the practice and I certainly needed the exercise, but I was far more interested in discovering a system of self-improvement and self-examination. I knew I needed to discover a sense of discipline, focus and purpose if I was going to stay clean—and to even stay alive.

I got hooked—and in the best, most healthful way possible. I became obsessed with the process of continual perfection and most of all, with the mindset of discipline and focus central to the practice.

To make a very long story very short, I eventually became an instructor. I earned my first Black Belt and opened my own school. Over a 30 year career I founded my own organization, Northern Chi Martial Arts Center, and grew it to include five affiliated dojos.

All the while, but especially after going independent, I focused the mission of my organization as, above all, a personal development program.

Self-defense is important and we always took the self-defense aspects of the practice seriously. But I knew there was much more the arts could offer, especially to people seeking some sense of themselves, or some system or process to improve.

Around the time I was celebrating my 20th year in the arts,

Introduction

I began to recognize a much greater application for the practice I had then dedicated nearly half my life to. My students were sharing amazing stories with me about how the arts and my teaching was transforming them; especially about how they were applying the philosophy in personal and professional life.

That's what led me to my current life as a speaker and author and how I started to share the ideas and concepts of the martial arts to help people become leaders—and to help leaders become better people.

This book is a reflection of that transformation. In fact, I started putting many of these ideas together very early in my career as a *"Sensei."*

I am a reductionist by nature. I wanted to simplify what had become a very complex and highly politicized martial arts world. I wanted to distill the principles of several styles that I'd been studying into a simple set of tactics that would work across any style or system and help people assimilate nearly any technique into their own practice, regardless of style.

I wanted to focus on the fundamentals—the most elemental parts that make any technique work.

As I got more deeply engaged in leadership training, I realized that today's leaders in any vocation face the same challenges as a warrior, a martial artist. I also realized that the same basic tactics and principles that make any martial arts technique effective worked perfectly in a leader's relationship with the people they serve.

As an academic study, leadership has become increasingly

complex. New understanding opened up by psychologists and sociologists have given us amazing new perspectives about how people interact, what they want or expect from their leaders and how leaders can perform more effectively.

The only problem is that somewhere along the way, we started losing sight of the fact that we lead people—not "human capital" or "human resources."

It's hard sometimes to avoid losing our humanity to process. Rather than deepening our understanding on a human level, we are too often seduced into relegating human behavior, needs, desires and ambitions to sets of data—to measurable outcomes, general trends, labels and quantifiable returns on investment.

Don't get me wrong, all these technical areas are important the management of any organization, community or group. You do need to measure productivity, the allocation of time and efficiency. You need to manage the ratio of the expenses associated with the people in your organization to their productive outcomes.

I'll state it again and this is one of the most important things you must keep in mind to be an effective leader...

You lead PEOPLE.

Every organization, every community and every company is made of people. It is people who drive systems and processes. People create and invent those processes.

The people you serve as a leader have very human needs, desires and ambitions. These needs, desires and ambitions

Introduction

require very personal and humanistic attention.

One more thing before we dive in...

Let's put aside the age old debate over "management vs. leadership," at least for the time it takes you to read this book. These are both equally important aspects of running an organization.

For now, just be open to the idea that management is about process and things, and leadership is about people.

Leadership is a deeply human expression. With all my heart and mind I believe that leadership is the most important and essential human expression. Leadership is the foundation of cooperation, and it is our ability to cooperate, when we're willing to do it, that elevates human beings above all other species on earth.

In this book, I'll share the most fundamental tactics that will strengthen your relationship with the people you serve—the people who trust in your leadership.

"BE A LEADER. NOT A SUPERIOR."

~TOYOTOMI HIDEYOSHI

Introduction: Musashi and the Original 5 Rings

Most of the material here is extracted and adapted from my longer book, **THE SENSEI LEADER**. I included a section in that book called *"The 5 Tactics."* Those tactics became the basis of an entertaining live demonstration in my keynote presentations, usually involving an unsuspecting volunteer from the audience.

Eventually, the *5 Tactics* evolved into a stand-alone session, often part of our half or full-day workshops. It is these *5 Tactics* we'll be exploring—these are the *"5 Rings"* that can help you become a more effective leader.

Working the *5 Tactics* with my workshop groups, I've gotten a lot of feedback on how these simple principles can be applied in real life and in the practice of leadership. Over time, I wanted to give them a little bit of an update.

And I wanted to create a short "pocket" book that you could take anywhere for reference or inspiration.

I've added some additional thoughts, suggestions for applications and challenge questions I hope will help you apply these ideas in your life as a leader.

A New Book of 5 Rings

Before we start, I want to introduce you to one of my mentors and the inspiration behind this book...

Minamoto Musashi is long gone. I have to admit that many of my most trusted mentors are, well—dead. All that means is that I can't talk to them. They can certainly still talk to me, to us—and Musashi has a lot to say.

Mushashi is best know as Japan's most revered sword master. He is that, but as is usually the case, there's more to the story.

If Musashi's sole claim to fame was how many opponents he vanquished or how many battles he fought in, it's likely that he'd be long forgotten by now. While he's revered for his expertise as a martial artist, he's remembered because he became something of a philosopher/poet and one of the world's iconic authors on the art of strategy.

In this book, I'm going to emphasize the "art" over the "science" of strategy and tactics. I could provide a lot of empirical evidence for why these tactics work, but that would make for a much longer and probably less interesting read. I want to emphasize how you'll apply these tactics in your daily life—subject to all the variables you face every single day. That's where the art comes in. You are the artist of your own life as a leader.

Minamoto Mushashi continues to be the living embodiment of Japanese warrior culture. His legend lives on nearly 400 years after his death.

As he felt his death approaching, Musashi retired to the hills to set down what he felt were the most essential principles of strategy and combat he had learned throughout

Introduction

his life and career. The result was a succinct distillation of warrior technique that has become today one of the most revered books on strategy and tactics ever written: *The Book of 5 Rings*.

The Book of Five Rings has been translated countless times in nearly every language on earth. It's contents are still endlessly debated by academics, military leaders, business people and of course, martial artists.

Part poet and all warrior, Musashi left behind plenty of questions and plenty of room for interpretation. Sometimes brutally clear, at other times mystical, sly and purposely opaque, he inspires each new generation of readers to wring their minds in search of what, for each of us, can and arguably should be a relentless and never-ending pursuit of self-perfection.

You might think *The Book of Five Rings* was meant strictly as a text book for the professional warrior. In his book, Musashi tells us directly that his understanding of strategy is just as useful in personal and professional life as it is in combat.

You might think *The Book of Five Rings* is kind of a Machiavellian work—meant to help the wolves fleece the sheep and now mostly useful to help powerful business and political types dominate over the flock.

It is anything but. Musashi clearly expressed his ethical heart. Of course to understand his ethics, we need to accept the context of his times as Japan began its incredible and often painful transformation from an extremely isolated, feudal and often bloody and brutal culture to a major presence in an emerging modern global society.

A New Book of 5 Rings

As different as Musashi's world is from ours, fundamental human needs and desires have hardly changed at all.

We still need leaders. We still want *ethical* leaders. We still want to believe our leaders are benevolent and act with our best interests at heart.

What has changed is our perception of who can and should be a leader.

In most of the world, you no longer have to be born into a Samurai class or its equivalent to rise to the highest levels of power and authority. Today's leaders are made, not born. More accurately, our greatest leaders today are those people who embrace whatever circumstances, conditions and challenges thrown their way and transform themselves into capable and effective leaders.

However—and with great respect for the historical context I mentioned earlier, we can preserve one important aspect of Samurai leadership culture that with slight modification, fits the needs of modern society perfectly—the ideal of *"servant leadership."*

The word Samurai literally means "one who serves." Today instead of serving a specific "Daimyo" or lord, we expect our leaders to serve us. Before we take one more step it's important that I share the working definition of the leader that I've cultivated over the past several years:

> **LEADER: SOMEONE WITH THE ABILITY TO ATTRACT WILLING FOLLOWERS—AND THE WILL TO SERVE THEM."**

Introduction

Again, the fundamentals have not changed much over time. Only the cultural context has changed.

Throughout history the best leaders have always been those who have shown the most caring and compassion for their people. I'd argue the most effective leaders are specifically those who have best served the people who trust in their leadership. Compassionate leaders—or at least those who can convince the people they are compassionate, are the leaders who enjoy the most loyalty and devotion and who can inspire the people to succeed in the most heroic causes and greatest adventures.

Of course if that compassion is not genuine, or if the leader's benevolence is nothing but a ruse to achieve selfish ends, that leader and the people in his or her care will inevitably fall prey to the "Authoritarian Slip" which leads to tyranny, despotism and dictatorship.

The only reason I raise some caution about the Authoritarian Slip here is because it can happen to the best of us. Many leaders slip into a dictatorial style with best intentions or in response to emergency conditions. It may be necessary to employ an authoritarian style at times. The problem is you can get stuck there.

The strategies and tactics we're going to explore can be used as effectively by the dictator as by the genuine leader. None of these tactics are inherently positive or negative. They can be used just as effectively for good or evil. It requires continual self-awareness and personal reflection to stay on the right path.

Musashi understood the ethical implications of his teachings. He purposely gave us a warning early in *The Book of*

A New Book of 5 Rings

Five Rings and provided a set of rules to keep us on the righteous path:

> Those who would like to learn my strategy should apply the following rules in order to practice the Way:
>
> Think of that which is not evil.
>
> Train in the Way.
>
> Take an interest in all the arts.
>
> Know the Way of all professions.
>
> Know how to appreciate the advantages and disadvantages of each thing.
>
> Learn to judge the quality of each thing.

Introduction

PERCEIVE AND UNDERSTAND THAT WHICH IS NOT VISIBLE FROM THE OUTSIDE.

BE ATTENTIVE TO EVEN MINIMAL THINGS.

DO NOT PERFORM USELESS ACTS.

Musashi's Book of 5 Rings survives as an iconic text for several reasons...

First, you can't argue that there was a cult of personality surrounding Musashi. The way his legend was propagated and promoted would make modern Madison Avenue marketers jealous.

I'd argue that the most important factor contributing to his staying power and his relevance in today's culture was that like many great leaders—he was lucky. Any warrior knows that luck plays a part in the game of survival, but that's not what I'm talking about.

Musashi lived in a very special time in Japan. He lived during a remarkable transition—the transition from *"jutsu"* to *"do."* That is, Musashi lived during a time when the Japanese culture was looking deeply into itself, and the 17th century warrior epitomized in the Samurai were leading this transformation.

A New Book of 5 Rings

"*Jutsu*" roughly translates to technique, but specifically the type of technique one uses in battle. "*Do,*" which is the Japanese form of the the Chinese "*Tao,*" refers to "*The Way.*" They were no longer satisfied with technical skill, but rather used the attainment of skill as a transformational vehicle for meaningful personal development.

In simple terms, this was the period where a skill like "*kenjutsu,*" or sword craft, practiced for battle took on another dimension. It evolved into "*kendo,*" or the search for the highest levels of technical perfection and spiritual development through one's practice. Battle technique was evolving into an art form intended for personal and spiritual development.

That's what Musashi wrote about and this is why his simple but profound text can still be applied today—even if your ultimate goal is something far removed from beheading your enemy.

Musashi was one of a new generation of warrior/philosophers in Japan. He certainly wanted to preserve his legacy, but he also wanted to organize his thinking on strategy and life before he passed. Feeling that his life was nearing it's end, and inspired by the request of his recently deceased lord, Hosokawa (Tadatoshi), he secluded himself in the mountains for a period of reflection that resulted in the **Gorin No Sho,** which means literally **Writings on the Five Elements.** This is what we know today as **The Book of 5 Rings.**

Musashi explained his intentions in a letter he wrote just before he died:

> "The lord asked me to write on the principles of strategy, but with the wish that he could come to understand

Introduction

sooner, I wrote succinctly. I wrote down my new way of looking at strategy without recourse to ancient expressions...or to traditional examples of martial principles. This is my original thought on the essence and the principle. I consider it to correspond to the way of the arts and of human qualities. It is a way that would be applicable as a universal principle."

Musashi was transcending the bonds of tradition and writing from his experience, and from his heart on the strategy he evolved and on the process of this evolution itself. This is one of the many reasons I find his work so relevant to leadership study today.

He understood well that what he was sharing would have application beyond the martial. He also realized that he had surpassed his teachers and had arrived at a new and different perspective...

"I continued to train and to seek from morning till night to attain to deeper principle. When I reached the age of fifty, I naturally fond myself on the way of strategy.

"Since that day I have lived without having a need to search further for the way. When I apply the principle of strategy to the ways of different arts and crafts, I no longer have need for a teacher in any domain. I do not borrow from the ancient Buddhist or Confucianist writings; I do not use ancient examples from the chronicles or the tradition of the military art."

A New Book of 5 Rings

In transcending the bonds of his tradition, Musashi was discovering a revolutionary way of thought for his time.

He was trained in the traditional techniques and strategies, but he refused to be restricted by them. In fact, his own father threw him out of the house for rejecting his traditional martial training as a young man. Years later, he came to understand the value of tradition as well as the importance of innovation and he reunited with his father, a renowned warrior in his own right, which eventually led to him founding his school of martial arts.

In **THE SENSEI LEADER** I wrote that you honor tradition by taking the best of it and building on it, not by allowing yourself to be constrained by it. That's exactly the process Musashi found in his own life and work.

Now before we dive in to A New Book of 5 Rings I feel compelled to share a few important points with you…

First—I'm not doing a commentary on Musashi's work. "The Book of 5 Rings" has been an important inspiration to me for years, beginning with my career in martial arts and later in my study of leadership.

This book is inspired, not bound by the structure, form or content of Musashi's work. Just as he felt the need to transcend his traditional training, I've reached a point in my life, coincidentally, at about the same time that Musashi did.

What I am stealing directly from Musashi is the goal that this work be succinct. I'd say—*simple*.

I am also stealing the way Musashi organized his book. I've reduced my strategy to 5 elemental tactics. As you

Introduction

understand these tactics, you can expand and apply them strategically to help you develop as a leader—and as a person.

And yes, I'm stealing Musashi's underlying intent. It would be more accurate to say that Musashi's intent inspired mine. Like him, I hope that my book will transcend technique and inform your process of personal development and self-discovery.

Like in the practice of martial arts, there may be some pain along the way. Expect it.

Like Musashi, I'm purposely leaving a lot of interpretation and application to you. You'll make mistakes—at least you should. Learn from them. Transform pain into progress.

Think like a Black Belt throughout this process. This means you need to practice, fail, question—then start again. Don't allow yourself to be satisfied. Keep testing and find new ways to improve and apply these principles.

Keep *"Beginner's Mind"* throughout this trip. Approach each new day, challenge and experience with a sense of wonder and curiosity. The mind of the Master is Beginner's Mind—hold on to this idea.

And as you become comfortable with each idea, teach it. Leadership is sharing—a leader shares.

You don't have to be perfect to teach others. You have to

A New Book of 5 Rings

be a step or two ahead. You'll learn more by teaching and sharing than you will practicing in isolation.

Just remember that like any good Sensei, you not only can, but *must* learn as much from your students as they will from you.

Welcome to the Dojo!

> "THE TRUE SCIENCE OF MARTIAL ARTS MEANS PRACTICING THEM IN SUCH A WAY THAT THEY WILL BE USEFUL AT ANY TIME, AND TO TEACH THEM IN SUCH A WAY THAT THEY WILL BE USEFUL IN ALL THINGS."
>
> ~MYAMOTO MUSASHI, *THE BOOK OF 5 RINGS*

5 Rings = 5 Tactics

If strategy is what you're going to do, then tactics are how you're going to do it...

I originally started working on these ideas to help martial artists. I was just trying to sift through the endless mess of martial art techniques, systems, styles and theories to identify the common characteristics of each one—mostly so I could steal!

Martial artists can and should be great thieves. Your development as a martial artist depends on how skilled you are at finding and adapting techniques that work.

Leaders should learn to steal good techniques too—and quickly. One of the great arguments we have in workshops centers on the vast number of leadership styles and types recognized by academia.

With all these styles and techniques to choose from, which is the best?

You could say none of them. You could say all of them. Fighting is situational. So is leadership.

Any strategy, tactic, technique or style could be the best in

A New Book of 5 Rings

any given moment. It's best to be articulate in as many styles as possible so you can apply the right technique or tactic in the appropriate situation.

This is why the metaphor of the "ring" works nicely. The "ring" or circle implies motion. It represents a dynamic application of tactics and strategies depending on current conditions and circumstances. Any or all of the 5 rings or tactics can be combined in any number of applications suitable to the reality you face in any given moment.

But that can be overwhelming. You also need to be a good janitor. Just as important as learning and adopting useful styles, you have to recognize which styles just don't work for you in any given situation, and trash them. At least for the time being! Holding on to a tactic out of comfort, security or emotional attachment can be dangerous—even deadly.

Keep it simple!

Martial artists can become addiction to complexity. There are a lot of "shiny objects" out there to chase. There's always someone peddling the newest, the latest, the "ultimate" technique or style. Of course, these are usually just recombined or relabeled techniques borrowed, stolen and adapted from earlier practitioners.

Today, this is a huge problem for leaders too. Every issue of *Harvard Business Review* or *Forbes* features the latest and greatest leadership tips. And just as in the martial arts, these are usually borrowed, stolen or adapted—the best of them anyway!

As I said, we are addicted to complexity. Complexity is attractive at times. Complex solutions seem more credible

5 Rings = 5 Tactics

somehow than simple answers at times. It seems sometimes that the simple way just won't get the job done.

Complexity can create unnecessary barriers to understanding.

Over time I learned that the most complex techniques, and later the most complex systems in martial arts or leadership, are made of and wholly dependent on a few fundamental elements. Identify these fundamentals, the "basics," and practice them, and you can apply them in rapid succession, under pressure or in the face of a complex problem or challenge.

That's what the Master really does. Look at any skilled practitioner in any art, science or vocation. You find people who are really skilled at seeing through complexity and focusing on the basics that work here and now. The more they practice these basics, the better they can put them to good use. Or as Bruce Lee said:

> "I DON'T FEAR THE MAN WHO KNOWS TEN THOUSAND KICKS. I FEAR THE MAN WHO PRACTICED ONE KICK TEN THOUSAND TIMES."

I learned that by identifying the basic elements of each style, technique or strategy, I could quickly assimilate new ideas and techniques. I was looking for the fundamentals behind any technique—the most elemental building blocks that unlocked the "secret," if you believe in such a thing.

A New Book of 5 Rings

Once you find those fundamental principles, they can be practiced and understood on a much deeper level. That's the irony—the deepest level of understanding is too often hidden or masked by complexity. And sometimes, sadly, that's intentional.

It's so tempting to make things more complicated. It can't be said too many times—*keep it simple!*

In leadership, the most fundamental, simple yet powerful principle you have to keep in mind at all times is this:

YOU LEAD PEOPLE! NOT PROCESS.

After thirty years I found that all leadership strategies and techniques depend on just a handful of tactics, that every martial artist must study and practice. As I started sharing my ideas to help people deal with life outside the dojo, I quickly realized these tactics are just as important and powerful for leaders. All you need to do is transpose these tactics from the physical to the interpersonal application.

Here they are:

- OPPOSITION
- DEFLECTION
- LEVERAGE
- BORROWING
- HARMONY

5 Rings = 5 Tactics

You may be tempted to add to this short list, and that's fine. But before you do, consider whether any other tactic or strategy you identify or develop just might fit into one of these five basic themes. I've been at it for some time now and I haven't found anything that won't fit into one of these 5 buckets.

Back to the dojo for a moment. I want to tell you exactly how I arrived at these particular tactics.

I started my martial arts adventure in a system called Shaolin Kenpo Karate. That name implies that Kenpo is a hybrid system—a combination of several traditions with contributions from Masters in many different cultures, but primarily Japanese, Chinese, and Okinawan.

Later, I became fascinated with Taiji, Qigong, and Chin Na. I also started training with people who practiced other systems including Tae Kwon Do, Shotokan, and Aikido. Just to complicate things even further, I decided to satisfy one of my "bucket list" ambitions and joined a boxing gym.

Believe me, I've heard some glorious arguing and chest thumping by one master or another about the superiority of this system or the other—this technique or that.

After a while, I came to the conclusion that I'd rather be the dumbest guy in the room.

That is, while the Great Masters pounded their chests and argued over which system, strategy or technique was best, I'd keep my eyes and ears open, my mouth shut—and try to steal what I could use from every one of them.

A New Book of 5 Rings

By the way, a lot of these ethnocentric experts were wearing orange and purple belts. It's funny how often the people with the least experience have the most inflated perception of their own opinions!

Fortunately for me, I found a few genuine teachers who were much more open minded. These Masters would look above the skirmish to see the whole field.

Dr. Yang, Jwing-Ming was one of the best. His background included a mix of various arts, both hard and soft styles. Even more important, he was trained both in traditional arts and in science. His doctorate is in electrical engineering which gives him a wonderful deductive capacity when it comes to understanding the arts and an ability to discern what is real and what is, well—crap.

I talk often about Dr. Yang as a martial artist, a teacher, and as one of today's most insightful living philosophers. In the bridge between East and West—Dr. Yang is the strongest plank!

He's a very strong plank in the bridge between traditional and contemporary as well.

Martial artists, like business people, often struggle with the desire to innovate versus a strong attachment to tradition.

Tradition is important, and it's vital that we honor and keep the principles, values and wisdom of the past—if it works.

5 Rings = 5 Tactics

We too often cast aside valuable tradition. Way too often we fall into Edmund Burke's infamous trap, "Those who cannot remember the past are doomed to repeat it."

On the other hand, we also too often cling to obsolete traditions even though we know there's a better way. Admiral Grace Hopper stated the problem clearly:

"THE MOST DANGEROUS PHRASE IN THE LANGUAGE IS, 'WE'VE ALWAYS DONE IT THIS WAY.'"

Innovation involves risk. Creativity requires courage.

Dr. Yang taught me to how to distinguish between vestigial and viable tradition. He helped me see beyond any one style or system and how to analyze the fundamentals that underlie all effective techniques and tactics.

I started to become a reductionist. If I could find the most fundamental elements of a technique or tactic, I could make it work in a variety of applications. If I could keep it simple, my recall and reaction would be much quicker.

As I've been saying, this works in leadership too!

In regard to techniques and tactics, I came to some powerful realizations. First of all, what we're ultimately looking for in any technique is *power*—our capacity to perform effectively.

The source of human power resides in body, mind and

spirit. If you want to be powerful, to perform effectively, you've got to cultivate each area.

You generate power through motivation and discipline over time. Yes—it takes time to develop power.

You apply power most efficiently when you master balance, focus and timing.

Understand these simple ideas, and you can find the power in any technique, in fighting or in leadership. Apply these fundamental concepts and you will become more powerful as a person. Learn how to share your power and how to help others discover and express their power, and you will become an effective leader.

Once I started to understand these fundamentals, it became much easier to understand, learn and assimilate techniques and tactics from various systems and teachers. If I want to access the potential power of any technique, I look for where I can isolate and improve balance, focus and timing. I find ways to practice those elements for each technique.

Isolating the fundamental elements of power in each leadership style eliminates any gap in understanding between the seemingly infinite variety of strategies, techniques and tactics.

Through this process I became more open and receptive to new ideas. This process also helped me evolve and mature to be far less threatened by outside ideas and other instructors.

(And yes—once again—this works in leadership too!)

As I became more confident and open minded, I started to host other instructors and bring them in for seminars so my

5 Rings = 5 Tactics

students could learn directly from the Masters. At one such event, I was practicing with one of my star pupils, Paul.

The guest instructor was teaching a leverage technique. Instead of being as engaged as I was, I noticed Paul was becoming agitated, even irritated.

I asked "What's up?"

"Sensei, all this guy is doing is Combination 3!"

Our Combinations are sets of techniques we teach to study and practice various tactics and situations. Paul had recognized the similarity between what our guest was teaching and what he was already practicing. The only problem was that he saw this as a problem.

I said, "Paul, that's great! Now that you see the similarities, you can appreciate the differences!"

Each master has their own unique twist on any particular technique. That's why we call them martial "arts." We should apply the same designation to leadership study. Isn't leadership as much art as science?

I continued, "If you couldn't understand where that technique is similar to yours, you wouldn't even notice the subtle differences."

I explained that most of the students in the room had their hands full just trying to learn the specific technique. It was as if they were learning an entirely new technique or concept.

They weren't.

A New Book of 5 Rings

Because they didn't grasp the similarity, they simply didn't have the capacity to see and apply any subtle differences—and those differences might make any basic technique or process more effective. As your capacity for observation grows, so does your capacity to elevate your technique and adapt your technique to a wider range of applications.

> ### "STRATEGY REQUIRES THOUGHT, TACTICS REQUIRE OBSERVATION."
>
> ~MAX EUWE

I've learned to look at any new technique by first identifying any core similarity with anything I've already learned or experienced. I isolate the fundamentals, then I study any differences to see if I can steal some new "chops."

This is exactly what I've done with these *5 Tactics*.

I've found through experience that nearly every technique I've learned in martial arts can be categorized under one of these 5 tactics. By understanding the power in each tactic, I can analyze any technique for its effectiveness and understand its most basic, most powerful application. Every leadership technique, every interaction you have with the people you serve as a leader falls into one of these tactical areas too.

With experience I've come to a point where I teach tactics far more than I do techniques.

The problem with techniques is that there's just *too damn many of them!*

5 Rings = 5 Tactics

Well—it's probably more helpful to say you've got plenty to choose from.

Tactics dictate techniques. Let's say I'm fighting an opponent much bigger and stronger than I am…

You can't fight strength with strength. Other things being equal, size and strength are great advantages in a fight. If someone is bigger and stronger, you've got to find a way to counter that advantage.

As you'll soon see, oppositional tactics won't work in this situation. I can't fight an overwhelming force with direct force. I've got to apply the tactics of deflection, leverage, or borrowing.

Within each of those tactics, there are any number of techniques available. However, if you apply techniques for force on force encounters to a situation that requires leverage tactics, they simply won't work. You've got to apply the techniques that best apply to the tactical opportunities in any given situation at any given time.

And you have to be ready to adapt and change tactics in the moment.

One of the great weaknesses of ineffective leadership is an unwillingness to adjust one's thinking—being close minded to change.

When you understand these fundamental tactics, you are better able to choose the right technique for each situation and adapt your tactics and techniques for changing conditions. Bruce Lee translated this idea nicely…

A New Book of 5 Rings

> "Be like water making its way through cracks. Do not be assertive, but adjust to the object, and you shall find a way around or through it. If nothing within you stays rigid, outward things will disclose themselves.
>
> "Empty your mind, be formless. Shapeless, like water. If you put water into a cup, it becomes the cup. You put water into a bottle and it becomes the bottle. You put it in a teapot, it becomes the teapot. Now, water can flow or it can crash …
>
> " … Be water, my friend."

What I've really done, like my hero and mentor Dr. Yang, is simply build a bridge. I discovered through my own experience that the same tactics that helped me access more power as a fighter also helped me become more powerful and effective as a leader. Teaching these tactics empowered others, which even further expanded my power or effectiveness as a teacher and as a leader.

As you practice these tactics and find ways to apply them in your life, I'm sure you'll get some bumps and bruises along the way. I certainly did.

Expect some pain. Expect to shed some blood, sweat and even tears. That's part of the process—and that's what this is.

The true Master keeps coming back to the basics. It's what we call in martial arts, "Beginner's Mind."

If something isn't working, maybe it wasn't the right tactic for the right situation—think about this.

It may be you didn't practice hard enough—or didn't practice properly, which is very often the case. Oh yes, you

5 Rings = 5 Tactics

can practice the wrong way and get very good at bad! Think carefully about that!

Keep looking in the mirror. Keep remembering that these tactics are the means—not the ends.

Adjust your expectations. As you practice, expect to learn. Expect to grow. Discipline yourself to reject any expected outcome. Successful outcomes are certainly the product of practice and application, but also of perseverance and sometimes even, dare we say it—*luck!*

I don't want to discourage you. Quite the opposite. I want to make sure you can maintain your energy even when the going gets tough. That means you have to acknowledge that the going will, at times, get tough!

Just remember that no matter how tough it gets, there is one undeniable truth...

You can do it.

THE 5 RINGS

> In matters of style, swim with the current; in matters of principle, stand like a rock.
>
> ~Thomas Jefferson

Opposition (Steadfastness)

The ancient masters said "stand like a mountain, flow like water." This is the stand like a mountain part.

Force on force opposition is expensive—in battle or in business! Still, there are times when direct opposition is the best option, if not the most convenient, efficient or desirable.

Know when to stand fast—when to hold your ground. Standing fast, standing in opposition requires weight and mass; sometimes massive effort and commitment.

In regard to values and principles, stand like a mountain. Unyielding. Uncompromising.

Steadfastness is expensive—but sometimes necessary. If you oppose a force of a thousand pounds, you need a thousand pounds to stop it. You need more to push it back.

What will you defend at any cost?

> No matter if he uses enormous power to attack me, I use four ounces to lead him aside, deflecting his one thousand pounds.
>
> ~Cheng Tzu, Taiji Classics

DEFLECTION

The ancient masters said "four ounces to deflect a thousand pounds."

Move—fade—pass—parry.

Instead of standing fast, you slip and dodge—redirect with a minimal force.

Now you're in a different zone—you see the opponent from a new perspective. You see openings that weren't apparent from the front.

Deflection can draw the opponent into a committed move that can be exploited. You conserve energy while your opponent expends his.

Deflection requires more skill—better timing—greater confidence.

What is the mother of all deflections? Think about this carefully—the answer may be in the form of a question.

> GIVE ME A LEVER LONG ENOUGH AND A FULCRUM ON WHICH TO PLACE IT, AND I SHALL MOVE THE WORLD.
>
> ~ARCHIMEDES

LEVERAGE

Minimal input—maximum power.

In physics and fighting leverage is using mechanical advantage to amplify input energy to produce and exponential increase in output power.

Not lazy—efficient. Leverage requires greater skill still—more finely tuned focus and coordination. Much greater awareness.

What does the opponent offer you? What are the skills, talents and abilities of those around you? How can you direct these forces with the most focused and efficient effort on your part?

Balance—focus—timing. These are the keys to leverage—and the secret to the efficient application of power.

In leadership, your lever is the mind—and you seek a psychological rather than a mechanical advantage.

True leadership isn't about having an idea. It's about having an idea and recruiting other people to execute on this vision.

~Leila Janah

BORROWING

What does the opponent or the situation offer you?

What force or energy is coming your way?

How can you draw this force—and then add your own?

Borrowing is the way of the expert—precise timing and committed response. Borrowing is the way of water the ancient Masters taught.

Be careful, though. In borrowing, you're not just floating with the current. You're like the oarsman rowing with the current or the plane stealing the tailwind. The result is an exponential increase in power.

Can you get everyone moving at the same time in the same direction?

Borrowing is the art of recognizing and exploiting opportunities to combine the energies of those around you with your own. Everyone united by a common vision to produce an exponentially powerful outcome.

You must be shapeless, formless, like water...

Water can drip and it can crash.

Become like water my friend.

~Bruce Lee

HARMONY

One with the enemy. One with the situation. One with the circumstances and conditions around you. Again, be like water—and be like the wind.

Wind and water can find the smallest openings. They can fit the shape of any container, and yet they are difficult to contain. The smallest breach can cause the collapse of the strongest dam.

Harmony combines all the previous tactics. This is truly "going with the flow." You operate in a state of active awareness where you recognize threats and opportunities in the moment and respond effectively, efficiently and naturally.

Harmony is the way of the Master. It is the way of motion, growth and life itself. Harmony is growing through the growth and development of others. It is increasing power by empowering others.

Harmony is not just going with the flow—it is the flow. The Master is one with this flow—not apart from it. Never ending. Ever changing. Perfection is not the destination—it's the never-ending process. Be a part of it.

The Commentaries

Opposition

Opposition

When we talk about opposition, we're talking about pure force—*mano a mano*.

There are two major oppositional tactics. One is the tactic of the bull—when you go head to head with the opposition. The other is to hold your ground—to establish and defend your position to the last full measure.

In a punch or kick or a direct block, our objective is to create a powerful impact force. We're literally throwing one object into another—like charging bulls. When two objects meet, the one with the most force wins.

Force is the product of mass and acceleration. The faster you strike and the more mass you throw at the target, the greater the force. You can increase the power of the strike by increasing either mass or acceleration—or both.

When you hold your ground, you're not moving at all. You've got no choice but to increase mass in whatever context that might apply.

Force on force opposition is expensive—in battle or in business. From *The Art of War*...

> "THE RULE IS THAT IF YOU OUTNUMBER YOUR ENEMY TEN TO ONE, SURROUND THEM; FIVE TO ONE, ATTACK..."

A New Book of 5 Rings

Sun Tzu is telling us that opposing the enemy by force is requires a serious commitment of resources. You need 5 to 1 odds to effectively throw yourself into a direct assault. You need 10 to 1 odds to effectively stand your ground against an entrenched enemy.

Despite how expensive or inconvenient it might be, sometimes you've got to go head to head and sometimes you've got to hold your position. At no time is this more important than in defense of your core values and principles.

In his book *No-Compromise Leadership,* my friend Neil Ducoff writes:

> "Tampering with the values of a business is much like tampering with the forces of nature. Compromise values anywhere in your company and minute changes, often called the butterfly effect, can cause a tidal wave of otherwise unavoidable issues, problems and drama."

Tactics are specific to particular conditions and circumstances. You must know when to flow like water and when to stand like a mountain. When it comes to values and principles, you are a rock.

When it comes to values and principles, the very title of Neil's book says it all—and I know he chose these words carefully:

NO compromise!

Opposition

Another area where direct opposition is the appropriate tactic is in dealing with bad characters. You've got to attack these enemies face to face. Hesitate to commit yourself to this fight and you risk losing the trust of good people who count on you to have the courage to stand up.

In our age of runaway political correctness, leaders too often placate the worst people in an organization—usually out of fear of political reprisal or legal entanglement.

Get over it!

Christine Pearson and Christine Porath present the butcher's bill in stark detail in their book, *The Cost of Bad Behavior*. Let's just start with this—according to their research, 12 percent of workers leave their jobs annually because they were treated with disrespect and incivility by other people in the organization, quite often by a supervisor:

> "Average price of replacing each of those employees: $50,000.
>
> "Annual cost of job stress to U.S. corporations: $300 billion.
>
> "Amount of time Fortune 1000 executives spend resolving employee conflicts: 7 WEEKS per year." *(Emphasis mine.)*

In one particularly compelling case study Pearson and Porath detail the efforts of Cisco Systems to analyze the cost of incivility in their company. Cisco is consistently rated as one of the best places to work—a model of civility! Still, Cisco

A New Book of 5 Rings

found that:

> "... the organization wide costs for potential time lost by targets who worried about additional uncivil incidents and future interactions with offenders totaled nearly $2 million per year. With estimates for the costs of weakened commitment (also calculated as lost productivity value) and job changes (calculated on the basis of cost per hire) added in, the total topped $8 million."

Pearson and Porath add that this is not the ultimate cost. It's just the "starting point" and doesn't include secondary costs!

You may not run a global corporation like Cisco. For the small business person, the cost in proportion to the total output of the business may be even more devastating. If you have four employees, what is the impact of losing one good employee because you don't want to go up against the company jerk?

The damage does not stop there. Perhaps the most disturbing is the cost to the individual. Being subjected to incivility and disrespect actually alters your brain chemistry.

"It seems that whether the snake is in the garden or in the next cubicle, flight or fight responses kick in." Unchecked, this condition can destroy your health. "Incivility may spark an effect similar to post-traumatic stress disorder."

This damage is lasting and, untreated, can leave an indelible mark on the targeted person's life.

Unfortunately, top performers and even bosses are too often the culprits...

Opposition

You must find the courage to oppose any bad actors in your organization. Sometimes you've just got to throw yourself in their path, force on force.

It is your responsibility as a leader to place the needs of the people you serve above or at least in equal position to your own. I'll argue that the needs of the people you serve and your own needs are one and the same.

In what other situations might the tactic of opposition be effective or necessary?

What conditions might leave you no other option but to stand your ground?

Deflection

Deflection is often more efficient and effective than opposition. In *Tai Chi Secrets of the Ancient Masters,* Dr. Yang, Jwing-Ming translates one of the *Taiji Classics:*

> "No matter if he uses enormous power to attack me, I use four ounces to lead him aside, deflecting his one thousand pounds."

Dr. Yang adds these thoughts:

> "If you try to make a sudden, major change in the course of an incoming attack, you might get bowled over by the forward momentum. Even if you succeeded, you would need to expend considerable force."

Imagine trying to stop an incoming punch.

A skilled fighter can punch with about 1,200 pound of force. This means that if you want to stop it dead, you need at least 1,200 pounds of resistance. To push it back—you need even more.

Just remember that a collision creates an additive result. Add your 1,200 pounds to your opponents 1,200 and you have 2,400 pounds of impact! That can create quite a painful physics problem.

Speaking of physics, I usually do a live demonstration of these tactics at events. I have someone punch at me and ask participants, "If this punch was thrown with 100 units of force, how many force units would you need to stop it?" Of course they answer 100 units. I then ask how many units I'd need to push my attacker back a step?"

At one event there was an actual physicist in the room. I asked him what the actual scientific answer would be. He stood up proudly and offered the definitive answer:

"More!"

It requires far less force to deflect the strike from the side, away from the direction of the oncoming force. How can you apply this principle in leadership?

One of the most powerful, effective and readily available deflective tactics available to a leader is…

The question.

A sincere, well placed question can deflect an aggressive attack and diffuse highly charged emotions. A good question refocuses the conversation to the aggressor's perspective, not because you're ready to surrender, but to show that you're willing to listen and try and understand.

One persistent challenge in leadership provides the perfect opportunity to apply deflection. It is when you're dealing with resistance to change.

One of the best techniques for mitigating this resistance, and one that is too seldom used, is to simply ask the people why, specifically, they oppose the change. Major changes are too often dictated from the top down with little or no input from outside the executive suite.

If you want people to "buy in" and support change, you've

5 Rings = 5 Tactics

got to start by understanding any concerns they might have. You never come to an understanding by proclamation—understanding starts with a question.

Instead of trying to get people to "buy-in," start by "askin'!"

Just the very act of asking sincere questions reduces the classic fears and insecurities associated with any significant change. Sometimes people just feel better when they know their concerns are heard and understood.

As you ask questions you may also uncover legitimate reasons for resistance that will help you avoid costly mistakes or lead you to a much more efficient implementation process.

Another useful application of a deflecting question is in dealing with an angry customer or client.

Faced with a dissatisfied or angry customer, it's typical for a service representative to respond first with opposition. Sometimes this opposition is supported by a specific return or refund policy, but there is nothing less satisfying to a customer as an excuse masked by an explanation.

Try this next time you're in the line of fire; just ask, "Can you help me understand, exactly, what would you consider as fair resolution?" Make sure there's no hint of sarcasm in your voice!

You may still have work to do to find a reasonable solution, but just asking the question throws some water on the fire. You're demonstrating to the customer that you have a sincere interest in understanding the problem from their perspective.

A New Book of 5 Rings

It takes a lot of energy to go toe to toe with an angry customer. It takes just a small adjustment in attitude to deflect that anger with a sincere expression of concern.

Deflection is often the most effective tactic for resolving conflict. Try this tactic next time you have to mediate a highly charged conflict between two co-workers, colleagues and adversaries.

Deflection buys you time—and nothing cools anger better than time.

Rather than fighting when emotions are hot, you schedule the match for a time when both sides can cool down, carefully consider their position, and debate the issue more calmly and rationally.

This is not surrender. It's a tactical redeployment. You're moving the fight to a more favorable time and better ground. You're positioning your resources to improve the chances of victory—for both sides. Sun Tzu would be proud.

To master the tactic of deflection, you need to become a good listener...

Listening is a skill. Like any other skill, listening can be learned and cultivated—and you've got to practice! I've coached many managers and business people in listening skills, and it all centers on one thing: *FOCUS*.

You can't force focus—it's a process of letting go. Most of all, you learn to let go of distractions.

The problem is that the human brain is wired for distraction.

5 Rings = 5 Tactics

It's a survival mechanism. We've got to learn how to control that mechanism and turn off the distractions when they're not necessary for survival.

Our ancestors evolved to shift their focus quickly. This quick shift of attention was very useful when they were hunting for their dinner and they heard the low growl of a saber-tooth tiger stalking them from the bushes.

These days, you're not likely to be eaten by a tiger while your attention is focused on listening to someone across your office desk.

When listening, your complete focus needs to be on paying attention to and understanding the person you're listening to.

This sounds basic and should be common sense, however there are a lot of distractions that can interfere with effective listening:

- *Your own agenda*
- *A particular desired outcome*
- *Actual environmental conditions (noise, interruptions)*
- *Personal opinions and beliefs*
- *Time constraints*
- *The urgency or importance of the topic (or lack thereof)*

The trick is to eliminate or at least mitigate as many distractions as possible. Once again—Simple! Not always easy!

A New Book of 5 Rings

Tangible distractions like noise, phones, interruptions, are relatively simple to deal with, but some distractions are not as obvious. I call these *"intangible distractions."* They're usually be a little harder to squelch.

Intangible distractions include:

- *Prejudices or entrenched beliefs*
- *Stress*
- *Outside pressures*
- *Fear or sense of threat*
- *Deception or lack of transparency*
- *Defensiveness*

Any of these conditions can steal your attention from where it belongs—on the person you're listening to. And there are plenty of others!

One of the most difficult intangible distractions to manage is—your opinion.

You might also say the tendency toward judgment or prejudice—and we're all susceptible. Practice putting aside your opinion, at least in the moment. When you're listening, your own opinions are *not* the priority. Productive listening is *receptive*, not *reactive*.

It certainly is difficult to keep quiet when someone says something you disagree with, however, the prudent time for response is usually later, after giving the matter some consideration.

5 Rings = 5 Tactics

When you show a sincere interest in listening, your considered response carries much more weight than a reactionary opinion—*whether you agree or not.*

One of the worst distractions is time—or lack of it.

Schedule time for listening. Your goal here is not a conversation—it's simply to make time to listen.

Make sure the other person knows in advance how much time you can commit to listening. This allows you to pay full attention without worrying about any other agenda.

In the moment you may want, expect or even need a specific outcome—that's understandable. For example, you may need someone to embrace a new company policy, or you may for any number of reasons need to make *this* sale.

However—in the listening phase, your desired outcome is a distraction. Practice putting it aside. Make your short term objective simply to gather information. This gives you the information you need to respond much more effectively.

My friend Dave is a Master salesman. The funny thing is, I've never heard him try to sell anything. I've been on several sales calls with Dave where he hardly opened his mouth—he just *listens!*

I'm sure there were times when Dave needed his commission to make the mortgage or put shoes on one of his six kids. You'd never know it.

His focus is always solely on his customer's needs—and he understands those needs by *listening.*

A New Book of 5 Rings

Not surprisingly, Dave is one of the most successful people I know, and one of the leaders I most admire.

I once heard that the greatest gift you can give another human being is your attention.

That's what listening is all about. It's about the gift of paying full attention to someone else.

Deflection is a powerful tactic, but keep this in mind at all times:

Do not use deflection as avoidance!

There's no benefit in deflecting simply to avoid important, difficult or challenging issues. For an effective leader, deflection is a means to buy time to plan the best response or a way to assure that cooler heads prevail in a crises.

If you stick your head in the sand, just remember that like the proverbial ostrich, your hind parts are still waving high in the air ripe for a good kicking!

Leverage

In both physics and martial arts, leverage is about using mechanical advantage to amplify input energy to produce an exponential increase in power.

In leadership, your lever is the mind, and you're seeking a psychological rather than mechanical advantage.

Inspiration and motivation are good levers for a leader. Through inspiration, you can leverage the skills, talents and energies of many people to produce a far greater result than can be accomplished by any individual working alone.

Opposition and deflection are almost always responsive tactics. That is, we most often employ those tactics in response to some immediate threat or attack.

Leverage, borrowing and harmony can be employed proactively. Be on the lookout constantly for opportunities to apply leverage and these higher tactics to innovate, create new opportunities, and expand the power of the people you serve.

Like a good Sensei I'm revealing each of these tactics in order of the increasing level of understanding, skill, and mastery you need to employ each one effectively.

It takes will more than skill to stand in opposition. It takes much greater skill to apply a leverage tactic.

A New Book of 5 Rings

Chin Na is the Chinese fighting art of leverage: seizing, locking, throwing and employing concentrated attacks against specific vulnerable targets. Much of what I learned about leverage, in martial arts and in real life, came from my experiences with Dr. Yang, Jwing-Ming and the study of Chin Na.

Dr. Yang wrote the bible in this style: ***Comprehensive Applications of Shaolin Chin Na.*** In it he says:

> **"CHIN NA MUST RESPOND TO AND FOLLOW THE SITUATION; TECHNIQUES MUST BE SKILLFUL, ALIVE, FAST AND POWERFUL."**

As I said, this tactic demands a higher level of awareness, skill and experience. You need expert focus and timing to apply these techniques effectively.

Dr. Yang adds, "It is usually much easier to strike an opponent than to control him."

Leverage is about control...

Dr. Yang told us about a trip he made to Russia to teach seminars in Chin Na and Taiji. One of his hosts on that trip gave him a ball cap with a saying in Russian embroidered across the front. It read, *"Pinky Collector."*

They were honoring Dr. Yang for his ability to control a much larger man by using a leverage technique against our smallest digit!

You can try this—*carefully!*

5 Rings = 5 Tactics

I'll state for the record that I am not liable for you injuring or maiming yourself in this experiment!

Anyway, gently pry your pinky back. You'll soon notice a point where this becomes extremely uncomfortable, then painful. Applied properly, you can lift a 300 man to his toes or drive him to his knees by the skillful application of leverage on the pinky.

I still use this trick in demonstrations all the time. I start by picking a large, rugged-looking guy out of the audience and asking: "Do you believe I can get this guy to dance on his toes using just one hand?"

Of course people are skeptical, but the physiology behind the experiment is really quite simple. By applying even a small force against an extremely sensitive part of the body, even a big tough guy becomes a lot more cooperative.

I'll warn you one more time! It takes some experience and skill to execute this technique properly without breaking the poor guy's finger off! ***Do not attempt this trick until we train you properly!***

In leadership, leverage is understanding and properly utlizing the talents, skills, abilities, knowledge and experience of the people you serve. When everyone is contributing, your time and effort can be applied efficiently. Leverage amplifies everyone's smaller efforts to multiply the group's power.

Earlier I said that wisdom is the combination of knowledge and experience tempered by awareness. Know your people and be fully aware of their capabilities, potential and tolerances. Be fully aware of the conditions and circumstances around you at all times.

A New Book of 5 Rings

In self-defense we call this situational awareness. Situational awareness is necessary in leadership too.

In fighting or in leadership, you've got to move first to employ leverage effectively. Otherwise, your adversary will read your intentions and either escape or counter.

Leverage also involves a concentration of force. In Chin Na, we attack specific, highly sensitive or vulnerable targets for maximum effect. Even a small amount of pressure or impact force applied in a concentrated area can produce a highly amplified result.

We call these sensitive areas "pressure points." In the human body, these are the points where nerves are exposed. This often happens in what we call body cavities, the areas not protected by the heavy armor of bone.

Once again, GENTLY take one or two fingers and fish for a spot under the hinge of your jaw where you find a very specific spot that feels less than comfortable. It's not hard to find!

We also exploit pressure points in the arm pit, inside the elbow and knee joints, and over the top of the sternum. The most sensitive and vulnerable cavities of all are—the eyes.

If you thought I was going to say groin, well, we go after that too, but an attack to the eyes is still far more frightening and devastating even if it doesn't carry quite the same mystique.

I'm very skeptical about some of these claims, but ancient masters even studied various times of day and seasons of the year where specific points are alleged to be even more vulnerable. The only two that made any sense to me were

5 Rings = 5 Tactics

to attack the stomach area just after mid-day, and to attack the kidneys and bladder early in morning. I'm only sharing this idea because in leadership, you certainly can utilize concentrated pressure more effectively if you understand the seasonal, daily or even hourly operations of your particular market, industry, organization and environment.

You can apply concentrated pressure defensively against an aggressor or competitor, or, just as with leverage, concentration can be employed proactively to expand the power of an individual and an organization.

Are you focusing your energies where they'll produce the maximum results?

Are you applying your talents and abilities to best advantage?

Are you efficiently utilizing the talents and abilities of others?

My friend and mentor Joe Calloway is the author of ***Being the Best at What Matters Most.*** On one of our podcasts I asked Joe about the power of concentrating your efforts for best results:

> "In business, the most successful aren't those who try and do everything. The most successful are those who do the most important things. Simplicity and clarity are *force multipliers.*

A New Book of 5 Rings

"Put your efforts and your intention towards doing those handful of things that are truly most important, and your success is sure.

"Don't overthink. Don't complicate. If you can make things simple, you can move mountains."

Give the man a black belt!

Leverage is about concentration and utilizing force multipliers effectively. Remember what the ancient sage Archimedes said:

"GIVE ME A PLACE TO STAND, AND A LEVER LONG ENOUGH, AND I WILL MOVE THE WORLD."

Borrowing

Physically, the most difficult tactic to master is borrowing...

Here's an example from self-defense. Instead of blocking, *(opposition)* you step inside the arc of a punch, intercepting the strike without diminishing or even deflecting it's power. Then, with expert timing and position, you turn your hips adding your power to energy you borrow from your attacker. You blend your power with his and ...

Wham! He's flat on his back.

This type of technique requires expert balance, focus and timing. You've got to master the control of two forces—yours *and* your attacker's. These forces can often appear to be in opposition—especially in leadership!

Borrowing is the art of recognizing and exploiting opportunities to combine the energies of those around you, plus your own, to create an exponentially more powerful outcome.

In our self-defense example, you borrow the physical energy of an attacker. Leaders can borrow energy from an adversary too—but borrowing can also be an effective tactic when you're dealing with entrenched opposition from allies, such as fear of change or resistance to innovation.

A New Book of 5 Rings

You can borrow from the people who are with you as well as those who might be against you. It's similar to leverage in that you're multiplying force by utilizing material and human resources to the best advantage, but borrowing involves a higher level of understanding, tactical expertise, and timing.

With leverage, you can literally jam a bar under a rock and pry it out. With borrowing, you've got to position yourself in exactly the right place at exactly the right time—and move in precise harmony with the forces around you.

In order to exploit these additional forces, you need to understand them. Let's again use resistance to change as a working example. Let's apply each of the tactics we've covered and see what might happen ...

Opposition:

This is the top down approach—command and attempt to control. Issue the orders and just make sure people carry them out. If they don't like the changes, they can leave.

How do people generally react under those conditions? What damage does this do to the culture and credibility of the organization?

Deflection:

"You've all done a great job and we appreciate your efforts and suggestions, but the company must move in a different direction."

5 Rings = 5 Tactics

Really? Does anyone truly believe that kind of statement, even if it's true?

Leverage:

A simple application of leverage would be to call in key players of your management team and representatives from the front lines and solicit their input. Now you're starting to leverage the expertise and perspectives of the people on your team to help ease the transition.

Borrowing:

If I want to borrow the power of my attacker's punch, I'll try to draw him into telegraphing the punch. I want him to throw a big punch—one that will give me more power to use against him!

In leadership—instead of waiting to respond to inevitable opposition, you proactively solicit input from those who are struggling against the change.

- *What is bothering them?*

- *What do they fear?*

- *What trouble do they see coming?*

Make it *personal!* Ask these questions:

"How will this change impact you?"

A New Book of 5 Rings

"How will it affect your performance?"

"How can you help us implement this change most effectively with the least amount of disruption?"

Create allies early in the process who will give honest feedback and support key decisions along the way, unless they see a better course of action, in which case you will welcome their suggestions and sincerely consider their opinions.

As I said, this borrowing requires expert balance, focus and timing.

Balance—Be well grounded and know as much about what you're proposing and the possible outcomes before you embark on any significant change.

Focus—Pay attention to all the possible implications and impacts and concentrate your efforts where they will produce the most positive results.

Timing—Engage stakeholders early in the process and adjust to any shifts, reactions or changing conditions and circumstances in real time, as they happen, throughout the entire process.

Borrowing is about getting all energies working in the same direction. This guiding force is quite often called the "vision."

5 Rings = 5 Tactics

The leader is the custodian of the "vision."

Sometimes the leader is also the author of the vision. At first vision may come from the founder. Later the organization vision can evolve to include input from many people at every level.

No matter where it comes from, the organization's vision should be a living thing—evolving and adapting to keep the organization relevant, responsive to changing conditions, new challenges and opportunities.

Vision keeps the organization, its processes and most important, its people all moving in the same direction.

Your application of the tactic of borrowing is much more effective when you can unite forces behind a strong, meaningful and authentic purpose—a *vision*.

Borrowing is the most efficient and effective application of your time, talent and skill and experience as a leader. Even the smallest input energy from you is amplified exponentially through the combined forces of everyone you serve as you get everyone's energy moving in the same direction.

The resulting output power is exponential!

Harmony

Harmony is simply developing your ability to combine and apply any or all of the other four tactics.

Harmony is truly "going with the flow." You operate in a state of active awareness where you recognize threats and opportunities in the moment and respond with the most appropriate tactic and technique—effectively, efficiently and naturally.

Be careful though! People love to turn simple but profound bits of practical philosophy into useless t-shirt slogans and allegedly motivational posters. "Go with the flow" doesn't mean you're just cork drifting with the current. It's not an excuse for ignorance, laziness or complacency.

Going with the flow requires Mastery ...

It means you've got the skill, experience and awareness to be in complete synergy with the conditions and forces in your space and with the minds and hearts of the people around you—both enemy and ally.

Harmony is only possible through Mastery.

Mushashi called this concept, *"Becoming your Opponent."*

A New Book of 5 Rings

You literally try to become of one mind with the people you're leading—and those who may oppose you. In the original ***Book of Five Rings*** Mushashi teaches:

> "In individual strategy, you must have knowledge concerning your opponent's school, discern his personality, and find his strengths and his weaknesses. Use tactics that thwart his intentions, and it is important to seize the initiative of attack by perceiving the rises and falls of your opponent's combativeness and by knowing well the cadences of his intervals. If the strength of your wisdom is sufficient, you can always perceive what the situation is ... if you accurately probe the mind of your adversary, you will find many ways of winning. You must work this out."

I hope you can now see why Musashi's writings are required study for business and leadership students around the world.

Musashi himself would say…

"STUDY THESE STRATEGIES AND TACTICS WELL."

APPLICATION

You're never going to know if it works unless you do it!

I've never been much of a fan of hypothetical training. In the dojo I learned early on that the best training was as close to real as possible. That's the only way to fully prepare to operate at your best under pressure, at full speed.

I also learned that every real-life situation was an opportunity for training. The key is to break it down—analyze...

What could you have done better?

Differently?

More effectively or efficiently?

And that addresses one of the main reasons that most "leadership development" programs fall short of expectations. With precious little time to divert from day to day operations, it can be an expensive waste to spend too much time working through hypothetical exercises when there are so many opportunities to train on the job in real time.

The process is amazingly simple, but requires discipline. Make this a habit and it will take surprisingly little time, yet produce lasting results.

All you need is a blank piece of paper and a few minutes. The next time you face a challenge—or an opportunity, create a heading for each tactic and write a short paragraph focusing on how you would apply each tactic in this particular situation, and what the likely response or results might be.

You can also do this exercise in review. Whether you've failed in a specific endeavor or you've produced some success, there are lessons to be learned—if you're willing to wring those lessons out of the experience. Most people won't.

Most people waste incredible amounts of time and energy wringing their hands and gnashing their teeth over a failure or a loss. Truly successful people don't—they quite literally pick themselves up, dust themselves off and start all over again.

And truly successful people never rest on their laurels either. As significant as any success may be, these people continue to look for opportunities for learning, growth and development. No matter how great the win, they ask themselves if they could have accomplished it more quickly, more efficiently, with less loss or with an even greater outcome.

Once you have your short analysis of how you might apply each tactic and what results you might predict, take a few minutes to consider how you might be able to apply a combination of tactics. You can sometimes apply multiple tactics to the same group facing the same situation. At other times, you'll apply various tactics depending on the personality

5 Rings = 5 Tactics

and culture of the sub-groups you lead.

For example, you may be launching a new product and facing some resistance. You may find that you need to apply opposition to those who are simply unwillingly to consider new ideas—they may have to go! You may find that leverage and borrowing are needed to inspire and motivate the design and marketing teams.

There are very few if any right or wrong answers. Leadership is as much art as science. The science is the study, the discipline, practice and constant re-examination. The art is how you respond creatively to the ever-changing conditions and circumstances you face as a leader.

And just to make it even more challenging, you've got a tremendous responsibility to the people who willingly follow your leadership. You've got to consider the impact of your decisions and your selection of tactics and strategies on the organization and the people who make it run, both as a collective group and as individuals.

Keep a journal of this exercise and you'll build an inventory of experience. You can then go back and compare actual results to your predictions and analyze on an even deeper level where you went wrong—and where you were most effective.

Document your experiences and eventually you'll have enough material for your book! All great leaders want to write a book someday, right?

Of course you can learn from the experiences of other leaders too. We have instant access to research, history, biographies and current news. In fact, we have more access to

A New Book of 5 Rings

information than any other generation in history—let's use it.

As I said just a few moments ago—this exercise is simple. Unfortunately, that which is most simple is too often the most challenging. I say this often and in many forms, but simple does not always, or even usually, mean easy.

Every complex set of martial arts techniques depends on discipline and dedicated practice in the most basic elements. Without this attention to the fundamentals, no technique can be effective.

Years ago I met one of the great Japanese sword masters of our time, Master Yamazaki. He told a short story about the process of becoming a Master.

He delivered the body of the story through an interpreter as his English is not as polished as his sword. It went something like this...

A student comes to the Master asking for the secrets to becoming a great sword master.

The Master says there are only 3 simple steps. Do these and you'll become a master. Ignore these steps and you won't.

"So," asks the student, "What's the first step?"

"Basic practice," responds the Master. "Now go away!"

The student leaves and practices diligently for 3 years. (I don't know why it's always 3 years in these stories, but so it goes!) He then comes back to the Master for the next step.

"Second step," says the Master, "Basic practice! Go away!"

5 Rings = 5 Tactics

The student leaves for another 3 years. He again practices diligently and tests himself with anyone willing to face him. Feeling very confident, he seeks out the Master to learn the final step.

"I've done exactly as you've said and I'm ready for the final step. I'm ready to become a Master too. Please, Master. Give me the final step!"

Now Master Yamazaki got his English on and finished the story himself. He belted out…

"MORE basic practice! Like Nike—just do it!"

It's exactly the same in leadership. Running the most complex organization effectively still requires disciplined attention to the most fundamental interpersonal skills, understanding of basic human values and most of all, strict focus on one's own development as an effective leader—and as a person of character.

We know what type of leader people best respond to. People are far more creative and productive when the leader cares about them—and shows it.

People follow willingly follow leaders who are Courageous, Compassionate and Wise—leaders who are competent and genuinely confident.

And people follow examples much more enthusiastically than they do orders.

This is not rocket surgery!

A New Book of 5 Rings

The problem is that too many leaders ignore the basics.

They get bored.

They let other things get in the way.

They fail to dedicate the necessary time.

Please pay close attention to that third excuse. It's the one I hear most often from leaders who are struggling.

At every workshop I do I ask leaders how important mindset and attitude is to their success and to the success of their organizations. How important are the simple human characteristics, values, and traits we've been talking about?

How important are the HUMAN elements of leadership?

Without exception leaders respond that mindset and attitude are everything and that nobody can lead effectively without prioritizing personal development, interpersonal skills and emotional intelligence.

They tell me that the human aspects of leadership are far more important than the technical.

And yet when I ask how much time and what resources they currently commit to the human elements of leadership, particularly their own development, the typical answer is…

None!

5 Rings = 5 Tactics

They tell me there are just too many other things to deal with—that they don't have the time.

They tell me how difficult it is to break people away from operations and management duties to focus on personal development or the human aspects of leadership.

You lead people!

Even in a heavily automated environment, it takes people to make the machines work. It takes people to manage processes. It takes people to invent, design, market and sell.

And it takes people to lead people—

Good people!

We all have the same 24 hours in each day. It's the same whether you're pushing a broom or leading a Fortune 100 corporation. Time is the great equalizer.

How you choose to use that time is probably the greatest factor that determines whether you'll be pushing that broom the rest of your life, or leading others to accomplish great things. How you use that time will determine whether you can maintain your role as a leader, or whether you'll eventually be replaced, discarded or deposed.

I respect the fact that as an organization or community grows larger in scale, its operations become more complex. There are more moving parts. You serve a much more diverse group of people with different agendas and means to achieve them. You answer to a broader and often more demanding constituency. You are responsible for more resources and assets. But the fundamentals never change.

A true leader inspires people to their highest levels of sustainable productivity, creativity and innovation, while the dictator wastes immeasurable personal energy and human potential on protecting turf and defending against the inevitable revolt.

It's completely up to you. Make time for the basics—or not. Be a leader—*or not*.

If you want to be a leader, and if you want to continually grow and develop as a leader, keep this in mind at all times...

IF YOU WANT TO BECOME A BETTER LEADER, BECOME A BETTER PERSON...

ALWAYS!

FINAL WORD—AND IT'S A WORD OF CAUTION

As you know, this short book was inspired by one of the world's greatest swordsman.

A sword is a powerful and dangerous weapon. It can be used in the service of others to defend life, liberty and our greatest values. It can also be used to cause terrible destruction. It can be used for conquest, exploitation and murder.

Your position as a leader is also a sword. Will you use it for good or evil? Will you use these tactics to serve others, or only for your own benefit and gain?

It is a leader's responsibility to apply and utilize these tactics not just to achieve your own agenda, but for the benefit of the people you serve.

A dictator applies these tactics as means to impose control—tools for fear, force and coercion.

A leader utilizes these tactics as means for continual self-improvement and as a way to improve the lives of others.

A New Book of 5 Rings

Be very careful. The tyrant can utilize these tactics as effectively as a genuine leader.

Let's review our definitions:

A LEADER *is someone with the ability to attract willing followers—and the will to serve them.*

A DICTATOR *is someone who imposed will or control through fear, force or coercion.*

Make no mistake, dictators can get things done too. Some dictators even justify their tyranny with best intentions. Some sincerely believe that nobody else cares as much as they do about "the people." They believe that they're operating in the best interests of the people they rule.

Tyranny is never sustainable over time and there is no just reason to oppress others, no matter what the short term benefits might be. Over the long haul, people will always resist oppression and will fight against it. Even the benevolent dictator, if there is such a person in reality, must expend a great deal of effort to guard against revolt.

Only a genuine leader—someone able to attract willing followers, can unlock the full potential of a group, organization, community or nation. Where a dictator commands, a leader inspires—and inspiration is a much more powerful and productive force than dominance or control.

What are YOU going to do?

5 Rings = 5 Tactics

How are YOU going to apply these tactics?

To what ends?

Are you willing to lead by example?

If we use a commonly applied definition of power as being your influence over others, these are questions you must constantly ask yourself. You've got to put yourself in front of the mirror on a regular basis to assure you're not going astray and that you're not falling prey to the Authoritarian Slip.

And remember always that who you are as a leader is most accurately reflected in your followers—the people who trust in your leadership.

- *How do they see you?*

- *Are you communicating effectively?*

- *Are they producing positive results, both for the organization and for themselves?*

- *Are you truly sharing power, authority and responsibility with others?*

- *Are you simply cultivating more followers, or are you developing more leaders?*

Seek honest and accurate answers to these questions and

you'll be able to determine whether you're genuinely walking the walk—or just talking the talk.

This is no secret. It's no great revelation:

You have a great responsibility as a leader...

Embrace the discipline of continual self-examination. It's your obligation to do your best to check your own ambitions against the context of the service you have pledged to others.

Ultimately, your effectiveness as a leader, your power, is dependent entirely on your ability to unite people in a common cause. Your authority is secure only when people trust in you as a leader and as a person.

The way to earn this trust is to lead by example. Be the leader—and the person—you expect others to be. This takes a lot of discipline and hard work. It means dedication to continual self-improvement.

People sometimes challenge me when I emphasize this commitment to self-improvement—to the never-ending process of personal and professional development. This emphasis on continual self-perfection can sometimes be seen as, well—selfish.

It is anything but. Improving yourself is the least selfish thing you can do. When you improve yourself, you become a much more valuable resource to others. Improve yourself as a leader and you are much more capable of improving the lives of the people you serve.

Improve yourself as a person and you influence everyone around you—one by one—and you may never even realize the impact you'll have.

5 Rings = 5 Tactics

It comes down to this...

If you want to become a better leader—become a better person. Along the way remember that perfection is not a destination—it's a never-ending process...

And it all starts with you. That's why you're a leader.

> "THERE IS NOTHING OUTSIDE OF YOURSELF THAT CAN EVER ENABLE YOU TO GET BETTER, STRONGER, RICHER, QUICKER, OR SMARTER. EVERYTHING IS WITHIN. EVERYTHING EXISTS. SEEK NOTHING OUTSIDE OF YOURSELF."
>
> ~MYAMOTO MUSASHI

The 5 Rings is available as a highly interactive workshop for Executives, Managers and Aspiring Leaders!

Jim's inspiring and engaging programs are perfect for your next conference, meeting or event. Programs can be combined to fill all your needs from keynote to half, full or multiple day events!

THESENSEILEADER.COM

FOR BOOKING:
BLACK BELT MINDSET PRODUCTIONS
207.751.4317

www.ingramcontent.com/pod-product-compliance
Lightning Source LLC
Chambersburg PA
CBHW070201230526
45471CB00002B/758